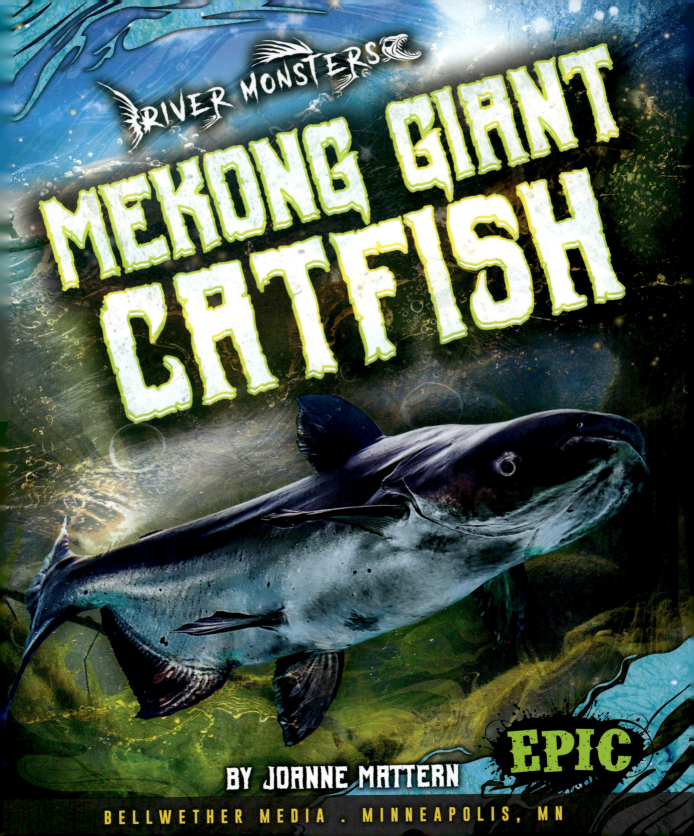

EPIC

EPIC BOOKS are no ordinary books. They burst with intense action, high-speed heroics, and shadows of the unknown. Are you ready for an Epic adventure?

This edition first published in 2024 by Bellwether Media, Inc.

No part of this publication may be reproduced in whole or in part without written permission of the publisher. For information regarding permission, write to Bellwether Media, Inc., Attention: Permissions Department, 6012 Blue Circle Drive, Minnetonka, MN 55343.

Library of Congress Cataloging-in-Publication Data

LC record for Mekong Giant Catfish available at: https://lccn.loc.gov/2023039903

Text copyright © 2024 by Bellwether Media, Inc. EPIC and associated logos are trademarks and/or registered trademarks of Bellwether Media, Inc.

Editor: Elizabeth Neuenfeldt   Designer: Josh Brink

Printed in the United States of America, North Mankato, MN.

TABLE OF CONTENTS

ONLY IN THE MEKONG......... 4
RIVER GIANT......... 6
ON THE MOVE......... 12
SAVING THE
   MEKONG GIANT CATFISH......... 18
GLOSSARY......... 22
TO LEARN MORE......... 23
INDEX......... 24

ONLY IN THE MEKONG

Mekong giant catfish are named after their **habitat**. They only live in the Mekong River!

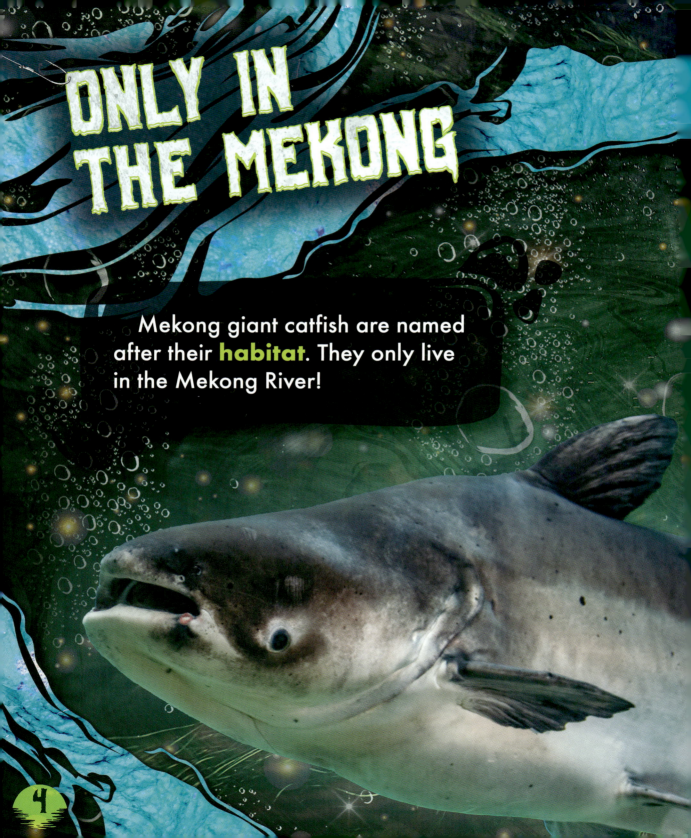

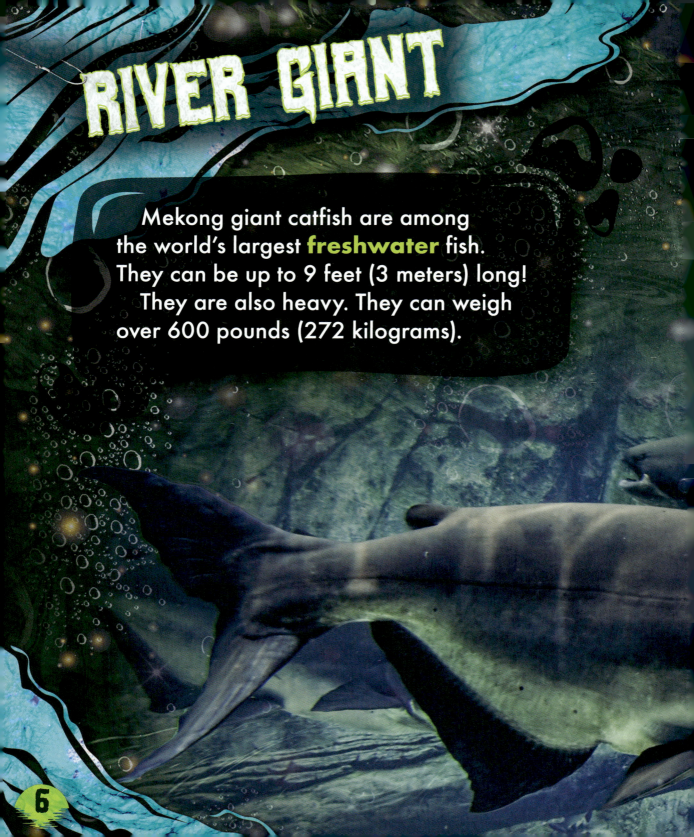

RIVER GIANT

Mekong giant catfish are among the world's largest **freshwater** fish. They can be up to 9 feet (3 meters) long! They are also heavy. They can weigh over 600 pounds (272 kilograms).

SIZE COMPARISON

AVERAGE ADULT MAN
Height: 5.75 feet
(1.75 meters)
Weight: 200 pounds
(91 kilograms)

MEKONG GIANT CATFISH
Length: up to 9 feet
(3 meters)
Weight: over 600 pounds
(272 kilograms)

These fish have gray and white bodies. Their skin is very smooth.

They have small eyes. Their eyes are placed low on their heads.

These fish have big mouths. This helps them eat food!
Young catfish have teeth. They also have **barbels** around their mouths. Barbels help them find food! They lose their teeth and barbels as they grow up.

ON THE MOVE

Mekong giant catfish live in deep parts of the Mekong River. They are slow swimmers.

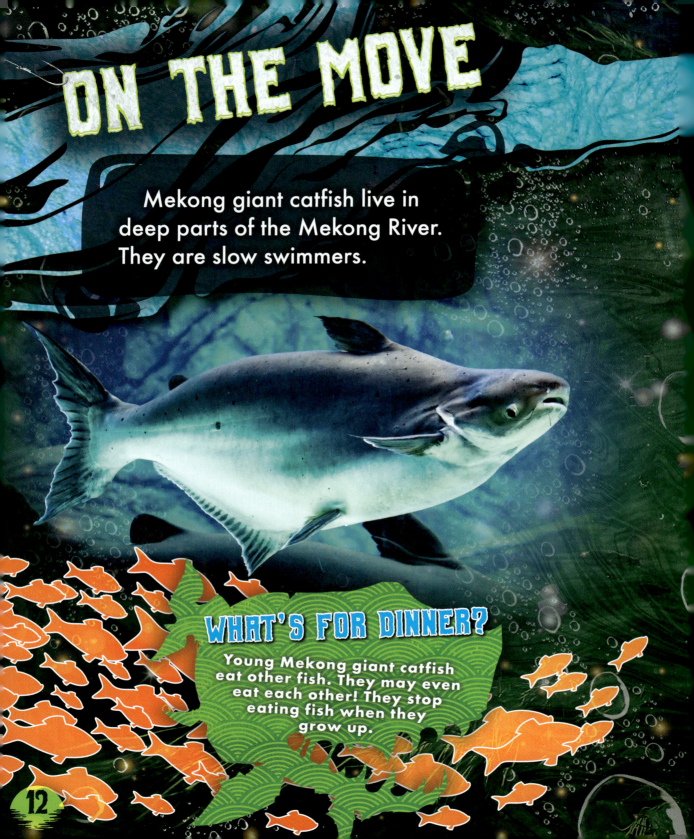

WHAT'S FOR DINNER?

Young Mekong giant catfish eat other fish. They may even eat each other! They stop eating fish when they grow up.

They suck up food along the bottom of the river. They mostly eat plants and **algae**.

These fish mostly live in the southern part of the Mekong River.

14

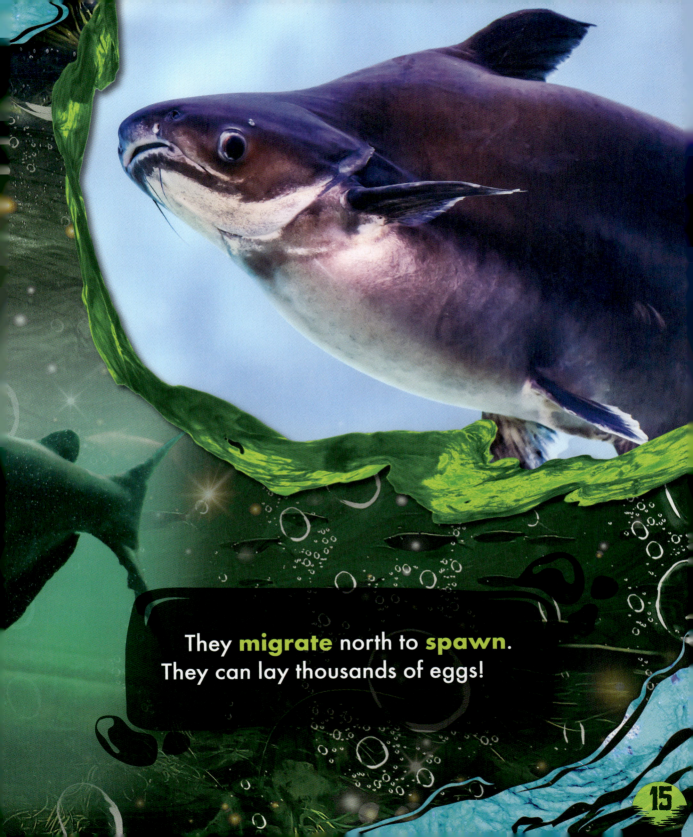

They **migrate** north to **spawn**. They can lay thousands of eggs!

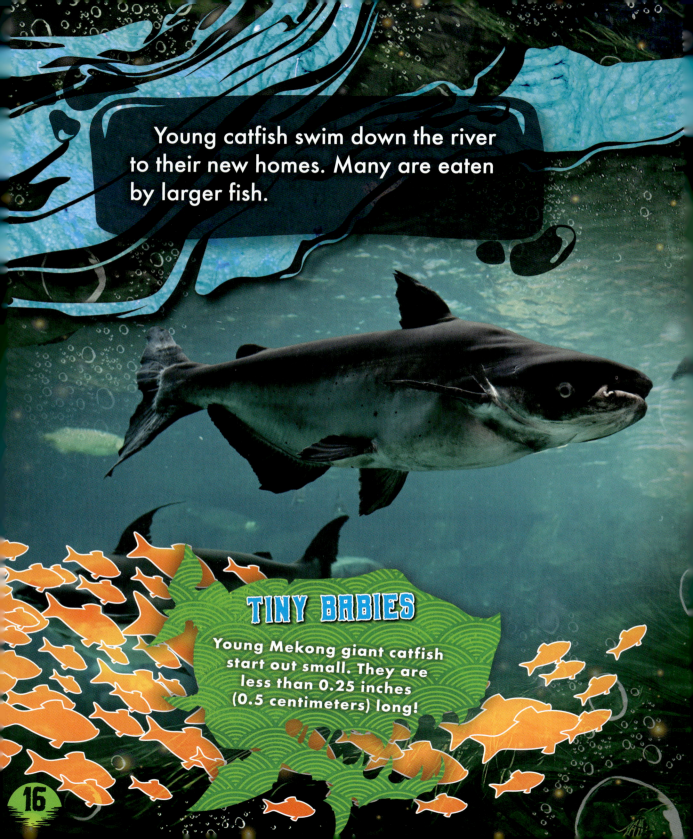

Young catfish swim down the river to their new homes. Many are eaten by larger fish.

TINY BABIES

Young Mekong giant catfish start out small. They are less than 0.25 inches (0.5 centimeters) long!

But young catfish grow up fast. They can weigh 440 pounds (200 kilograms) in six years!

RECORD CATCH

0 feet
2 feet
4 feet
6 feet
8 feet
10 feet

WEIGHT
646 pounds
(293 kilograms)

LENGTH
9 feet
(3 meters)

WHEN WAS IT CAUGHT?
May 1, 2005

WHERE WAS IT CAUGHT?
Mekong River, Thailand

17

SAVING THE MEKONG GIANT CATFISH

Long ago, there were many giant catfish. Today, they are **critically endangered**. They are in danger because of **overfishing** and **pollution**. They are losing their habitats, too. Dams stop them from spawning.

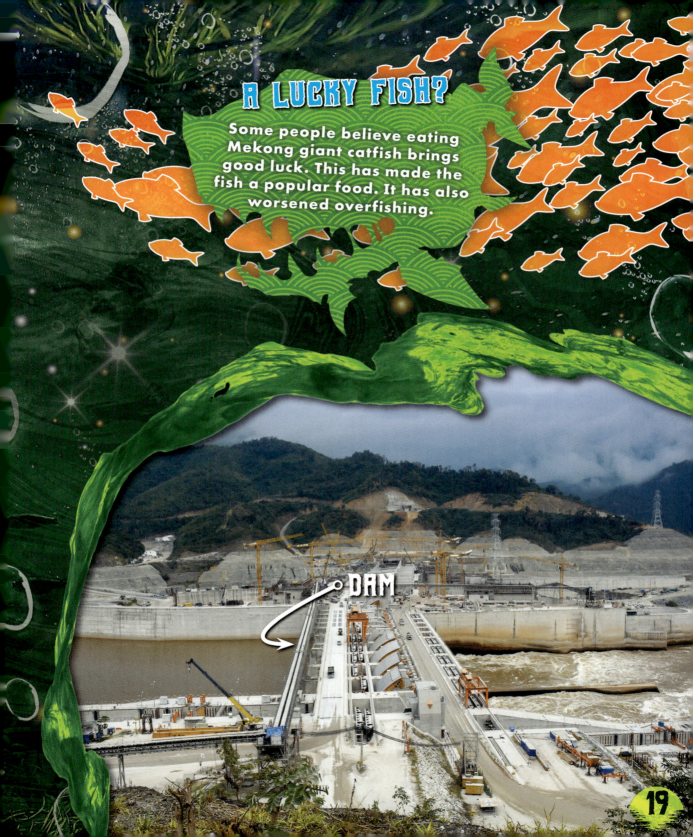

A LUCKY FISH?

Some people believe eating Mekong giant catfish brings good luck. This has made the fish a popular food. It has also worsened overfishing.

DAM

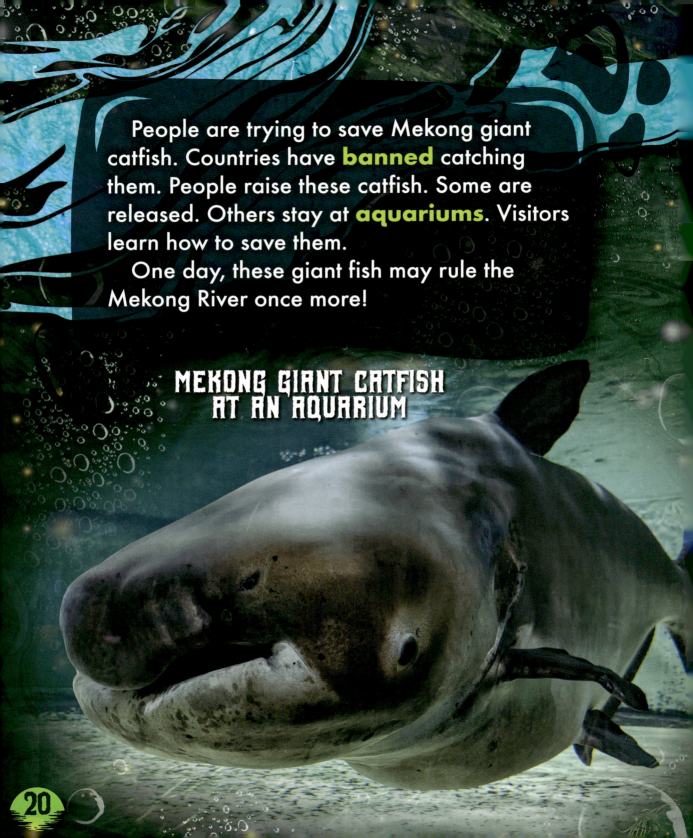

People are trying to save Mekong giant catfish. Countries have **banned** catching them. People raise these catfish. Some are released. Others stay at **aquariums**. Visitors learn how to save them.

One day, these giant fish may rule the Mekong River once more!

MEKONG GIANT CATFISH AT AN AQUARIUM

MEKONG GIANT CATFISH STATS

| LEAST CONCERN | NEAR THREATENED | VULNERABLE | ENDANGERED | CRITICALLY ENDANGERED | EXTINCT IN THE WILD | EXTINCT |

LIFE SPAN
up to 60 years

THREATS
overfishing, pollution, habitat loss

MEKONG GIANT CATFISH BEING RELEASED INTO THE WILD

GLOSSARY

algae—plants and plantlike living things; most kinds of algae grow in water.

aquariums—buildings where people can see and learn about fish and other underwater creatures

banned—made something against the law

barbels—whiskers on some fish that help them sense their surroundings

critically endangered—greatly in danger of dying out

freshwater—related to water that is not salty

habitat—a place where an animal lives

migrate—to move from one place to another, often with the seasons

overfishing—using up the number of fish by fishing too much

pollution—substances that make nature dirty and unsafe

spawn—to lay eggs